LET'S FIND OUT! PHYSICAL SCIENCE

WHAT IS FRICTION?

LISA IDZIKOWSKI

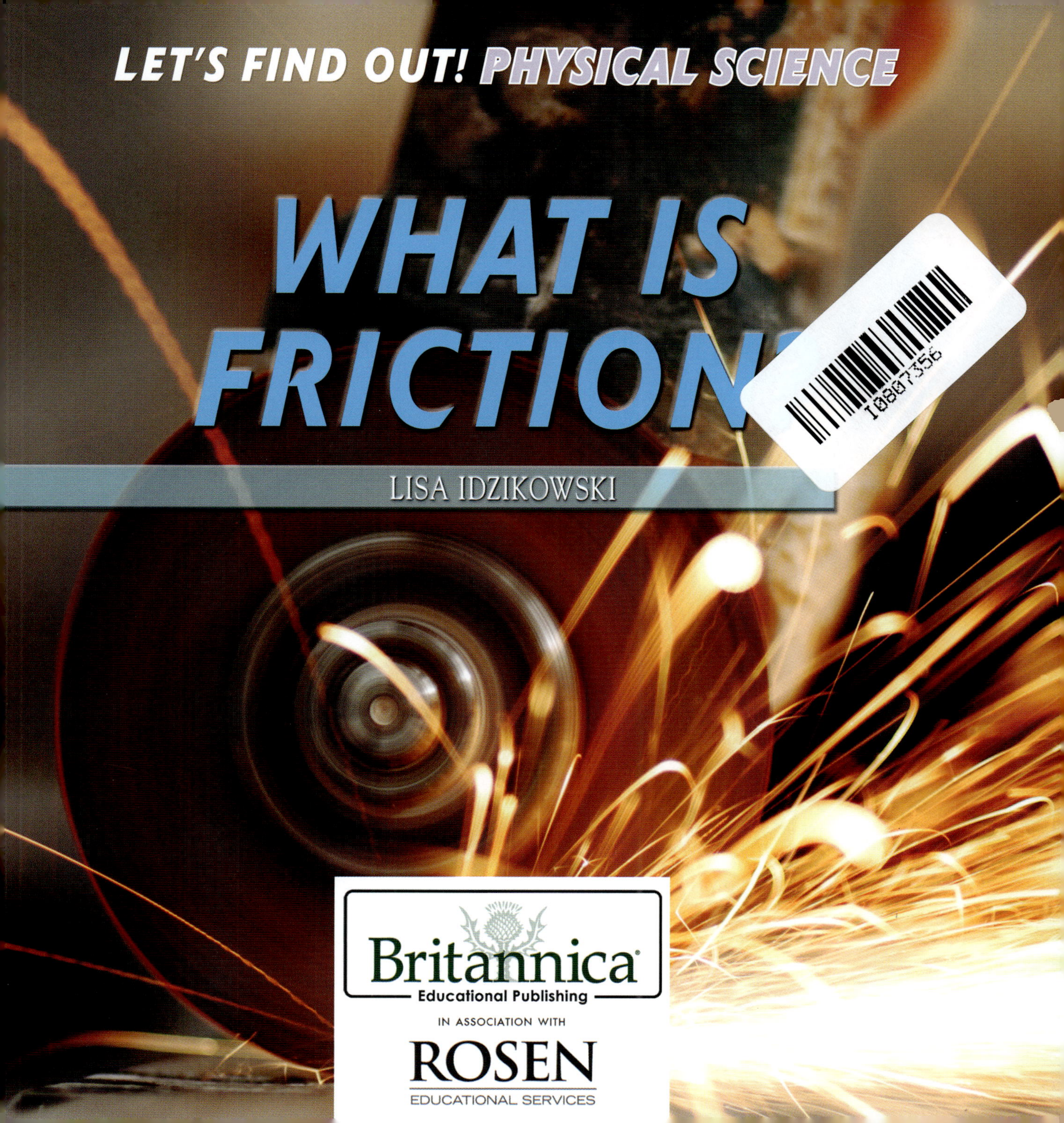

Britannica Educational Publishing
IN ASSOCIATION WITH
ROSEN
EDUCATIONAL SERVICES

Published in 2015 by Britannica Educational Publishing (a trademark of Encyclopædia Britannica, Inc.) in association with The Rosen Publishing Group, Inc.
29 East 21st Street, New York, NY 10010

Distributed exclusively by Rosen Publishing.
To see additional Britannica Educational Publishing titles, go to rosenpublishing.com.

First Edition

Britannica Educational Publishing
J.E. Luebering: Director, Core Reference Group
Mary Rose McCudden: Editor, Britannica Student Encyclopedia

Rosen Publishing
Hope Lourie Killcoyne: Executive Editor
Andrea Sclarow Paskoff: Editor
Nelson Sá: Art Director
Nelson Sá and Brian Garvey: Designers
Cindy Reiman: Photography Manager
Marty Levick: Photo Researcher

Cataloging-in-Publication Data

Idzikowski, Lisa.
What is friction?/by Lisa Idzikowski.
p. cm.—(Let's find out! Physical science)
Includes bibliographical references and index.
ISBN 978-1-6227-5502-8 (library binding)—ISBN 978-1-6227-5504-2 (pbk.)—ISBN 978-1-6227-5505-9 (6-pack)
1. Friction—Juvenile literature. I. Idzikowski, Lisa. II. Title.
QC197.I39 2015
531—d23

Manufactured in the United States of America.

Photo Credits: Cover, p. 1 Yellowj/Shutterstock.com; p. 4 TommL/Vetta/Getty Images; p. 5 Ivica Drusany/Shutterstock.com; pp. 6–7 Boston Museum of Science/Visuals Unlimited/Getty Images; p. 7 Yarinca/E+/Getty Images; p. 8 Denkou Images/Cultura/Getty Images; p. 9 *Procycling* Magazine/Future/Getty Images; p. 10 tammykayphoto/Shutterstock.com; p. 11 Vaclav Volrab/Shutterstock.com; p. 12 Joel Saget/AFP/Getty Images; pp. 12–13 Calvin Chan/Shutterstock.com; p. 14 © iStockphoto.com/stevecoleimages; p. 15 snig/Shutterstock.com; pp. 16–17 Rob Carr/Getty Images; p. 17 imagebroker.net/SuperStock; p. 18 Getty Images; p. 19 © iStockphoto.com/ppart; p. 20 Levent Konuk/Shutterstock.com; p. 21 © Comstock/Thinkstock; pp. 22–23 (top) brave rabbit/Shutterstock.com; pp. 22–23 (bottom) Dejan Milinkovic/Thinkstock; pp. 24–25 Biophoto Associates/Science Source; p. 25 BIOphotos/Shutterstock.com; pp. 26–27 (top) Werner Lang/imagebroker.net/SuperStock; pp. 26–27 (bottom) Maksym Gorpenyuk/Shutterstock.com; pp. 28–29 Rich Legg/E+/Getty Images; p. 29 James Gerholdt/Photolibrary/Getty Images; interior page borders KConstantine/Shutterstock.com.

Contents

Friction Is Everywhere

Friction is everywhere. It is a force (a push or pull) that acts between two objects that are touching one another. Friction slows or stops the movement between the surfaces of the objects that are touching.

Gliding over snow is possible because wax on the skis reduces friction between the skis and the snow.

Think About It

Friction occurs between all types of matter. Name two solids, a solid and a liquid, or a solid and a gas. How could they come into contact?

Friction can occur between all types of matter: solids, liquids, and gases. Sometimes it can be useful. At other times it can cause problems. All around us—at home, at school, at work, and at play—we encounter friction in our lives every day.

A parachute creates friction with air to slow a skydiver.

Look Closely

Scientists use microscopes to look closely at all kinds of things. When they look at the surfaces of common objects, all sorts of tiny bumps, ridges, and pits show up. What about glass or slippery plastic? Looking carefully shows that this is true for even the smoothest of surfaces.

Under a microscope, an adhesive bandage has all kinds of bumps and jagged edges.

Plain wooden floors have little friction to stop toy cars.

When objects touch or rub together, the bumps, ridges, and pits grip, grind, drag, and smash into each other. Rough surfaces, such as a carpeted floor, have more of these bumps and jagged edges. They produce a larger amount of friction. Smoother surfaces, such as a plain wood floor, are more even. They produce less friction.

Compare and Contrast

Compare and contrast what could happen while playing with toys like cars or marbles on different types of floors.

Friction Is Useful

At home, at school, and even outside on the sidewalk, events depend on the helpful effects of friction. When people walk, friction between the soles of their shoes and the ground prevents them from slipping and sliding.

Think About It

Friction produces heat. Why might someone rub his or her hands together on a cold day?

The treads on hiking boots prevent hikers from slipping and sliding on rocks.

Bike brake pads create friction with the wheel rim to stop a bike.

Imagine getting to school and not being able to draw, write, or color. Without friction, it would be impossible to grip your pencils, pens, or crayons, and they would not be able to mark the paper.

It may be fun and exciting to go fast on a bike, but eventually you will need to stop. Friction between the brakes and the wheels slows down and finally stops the bike.

FRICTION IS FUN

How do you have fun at the park or playground? Baseball is fun to play during the summer. A tip-top baseball player needs to grip the bat, hit the ball, and run rapidly. How about playing tag? It is exciting to run, turn, or stop quickly. These activities are possible with enough friction between your hands and the bat and between your shoes and the ground.

Friction helps you grip the bat. Then you can keep your eye on the ball and swing.

Swimming and sledding are fun, too. Splashing down a slippery slide into a pool is delightful on a warm day, and zipping down a snowy hill in winter is thrilling. Going fast down the slide or the hill is possible because the smooth plastic surface and the snowy ground create little friction.

Think About It
Explain how an activity you enjoy depends on friction.

The low-friction plastic of a sled makes for a fast ride.

Friction Can Increase Safety

There are many ways that friction can improve safety inside and outside our homes and schools. During winter, when it is cold outside, streets and sidewalks may become icy and slippery. People try to melt the ice. They also throw sand on top of it. This increases the friction between their shoes or boots and the icy

People toss sand onto icy walkways to increase friction.

surface. Better friction decreases the chances of slipping and falling.

In the shower, bathtub, and other wet areas, water decreases the friction between people's feet and the surface they are stepping on. What's the solution? Use a rubber mat to increase the friction and prevent accidental slips and falls.

Compare and Contrast

What is done to the rungs of a ladder to increase safety? How does this compare to using a rubber mat in a wet area?

Mats placed around public swimming pools increase friction to prevent slipping and falling.

Not All Friction Is the Same

Friction occurs when two objects are in contact with one another. If there is no movement between the objects, it is known as static friction.

Think About It
Describe a time when static friction made it hard to get a job done.

Think about someone who is cleaning his or her bedroom. In the middle of the room is

Moving an object by overcoming static friction is not easy, especially on an incline.

Heavy objects like cars require lots of force to get going.

a large box filled with toys. To finish the job, the box needs to be pushed into the closet. But it won't be easy. Static friction between the floor and the bottom of the box holds it in place. If the box gets heavier, the amount of static friction increases. In order to move the box, it will have to be pushed harder to overcome the static friction.

Another Type of Friction

Static friction occurs when two objects are in contact with one another and there is no movement. Kinetic friction happens when two things are moving or sliding against one another. Kinetic friction resists an object that is moving or sliding, eventually bringing it to a stop.

Kinetic friction slows a baseball player sliding into a base.

Once the sled gets going, it is easier for the dogs to keep moving.

THINK ABOUT IT

When you need to push a heavy object to a certain point, is it better to stop and take rests or try to keep going once you have started moving it?

Think back to the person with the large, toy-filled box. Once the person gets the box moving, it is not as difficult to push and slide it along the floor. The person will notice that it takes less effort to push against kinetic friction and keep the box going than it does to get the box moving in the first place.

Just How Much?

Just how much friction is produced by the surfaces of certain things? With some substances, more friction will occur. With others, less friction will occur. The amount of friction created by different surfaces can be measured. This measurement is called the **coefficient** of friction.

Surfaces that slow down movement the most are high

Some athletes wear suits specially designed to decrease friction while swimming.

The **coefficient** of friction is a measure of how easily one object moves in relation to another.

friction. Sliding a concrete brick over a concrete road would be terribly difficult. So concrete is said to have a high coefficient of friction. Surfaces that allow more movement to occur have lower friction. Cooked foods slide easily over a pan coated with a material with a low coefficient of friction.

Many frying pans are made with surfaces that keep foods from sticking.

Too Much Friction Can Cause Problems

Sometimes friction causes problems. Too much can be harmful for machinery. Many parts in the engines of cars experience a lot of friction. This can cause those parts to wear down and possibly break. **Lubricants** such as oil and grease are applied to these moving parts to decrease the amount of friction and help solve the problem.

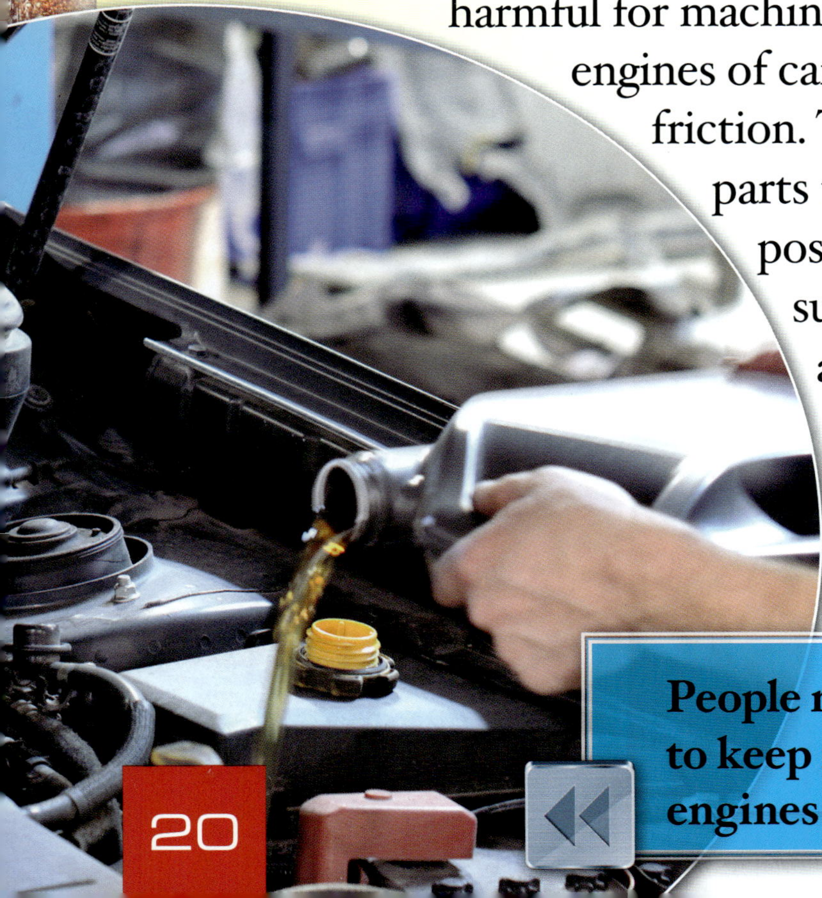

People must add oil, a lubricant, to keep moving parts inside car engines from becoming damaged.

A **lubricant** is a substance used to decrease friction between surfaces that are in contact.

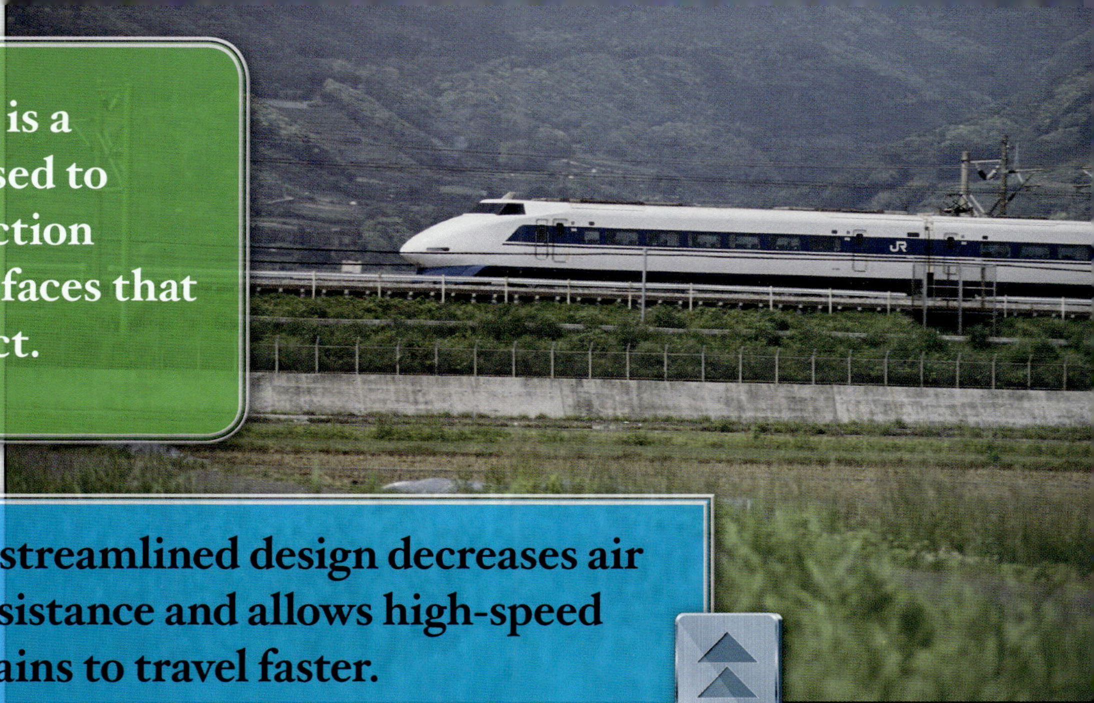

A streamlined design decreases air resistance and allows high-speed trains to travel faster.

Objects also move through air. The air pushes against the object as it moves, slowing it down. This type of friction is known as air resistance. The bodies of birds are naturally round and smooth. This decreases air resistance, helping them fly. Airplanes, rockets, and high-speed trains are designed with the same kinds of rounded shapes. This kind of design, known as streamlining, helps vehicles move more easily through the air.

Too Little Friction Can Cause Problems

At times, too little friction can cause problems. In order for an airplane to land safely, the pilot sets the plane's flaps in the correct position. Air pushing against the flaps, or air resistance, allows the plane to slow down. Without the flaps, the plane would land at a

Pilots depend on air resistance in order to slow down and safely land their airplanes.

THINK ABOUT IT

What could happen if the treads on your bicycle tires are worn down?

Race car drivers depend on high-friction tires to give them control on the racetrack.

higher speed and need a much longer runway to slow down and stop.

Car tires have treads to increase the amount of friction between the tires and the road. If the treads are worn down, this creates too little friction. The car may slip and spin out of control on wet, slippery roads.

Racing cars have tires that are made extra wide. A larger amount of tire surface makes contact with the road. This increases friction, which gives the race-car driver better control over the car.

FRICTION IN NATURE

Friction also affects animals. Snails and snakes creep and slither along the ground. Rocks and sticks may make it tough for them to travel. Snails have solved this. They produce their own natural lubricant, a slippery substance called mucus. The mucus allows the snail

Snails produce mucus, a natural lubricant that helps them to crawl.

to glide wherever it needs to go. Snakes use the friction created by their scales to slither through their surroundings.

Animals that live in the water deal with **water resistance**. Many fish and other underwater creatures have rounded heads and bodies. Others have long, slim heads and bodies. These shapes decrease water resistance, allowing them to swim underwater more easily.

Water resistance is friction that affects objects moving through water.

Animals that live underwater are often shaped to reduce friction in the water.

Friction's Special Effects

Friction produces special effects. The friction caused by two objects rubbing or sliding against one another creates heat. By rubbing two sticks together, it is possible to make enough heat to start a fire.

Many cultures have long known how to start a fire with heat from friction.

Quite often, chunks of rock and other materials from space enter Earth's atmosphere. These meteors travel so fast that the friction between the meteor and the atmosphere produces an extreme amount of heat. As a result, the surface of the meteor melts and burns. We see this as a light in the night sky known as a shooting star.

Many insects communicate by rubbing body parts together.

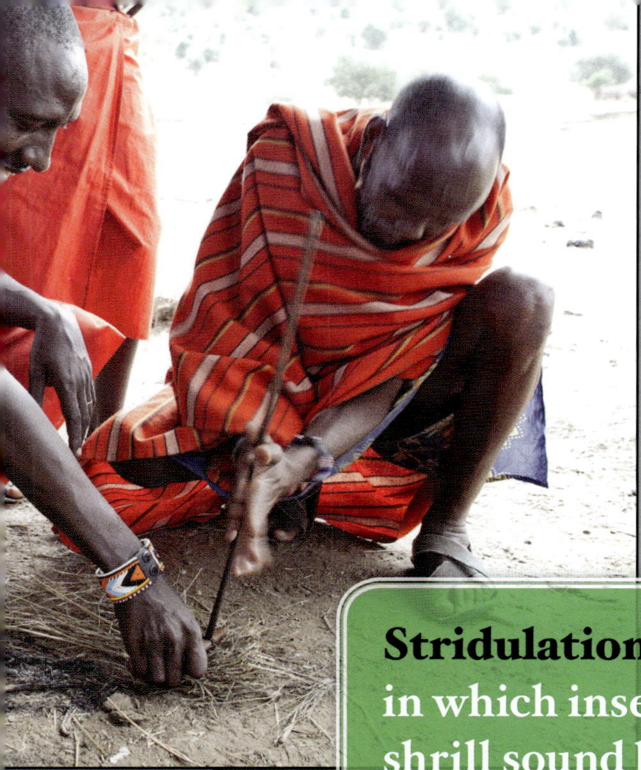

What would a warm summer evening be without chirping crickets? The chirping sound is made when the cricket rubs its wings together, an act known as **stridulation**.

Stridulation is a process in which insects make a shrill sound by rubbing two body parts together.

Friction's Effects Are All Around

Friction is a very important part of our lives. In our neighborhoods and communities, people of all ages use friction for their work and play. It is a force that cannot be seen, but its effects can be felt and observed. It will always be with us.

Today and in the future, engineers will continue to learn

Rock climbing is made safe by the use of a safety harness and the friction provided by good climbing shoes.

Think About It

What do you think may be manufactured in the future because of friction?

about friction. They will create products that use the helpful effects of friction. And they will solve problems that occur when there is too much friction.

Many animals have feet that provide friction for locomotion.

Glossary

air resistance The force that air exerts on an object moving through it.

engineers People who design and build complicated products, machines, systems, or structures.

force An influence, such as a push or pull, that produces a change in the speed or direction of an object's motion.

friction A force that resists motion between two objects that are in contact with one another.

heat A form of energy that causes substances to rise in temperature.

kinetic friction A force that resists the motion of two objects that are sliding against one another.

liquid A substance, such as water or oil, that flows freely but takes up a definite amount of space.

manufactured Made by machinery or by hand.

meteors Pieces of rock or metal that fall from space into Earth's atmosphere, where the heat of friction causes them to burn and glow brightly in the sky.

microscopes Instruments used for producing enlarged images of very small objects so that they can be seen clearly.

mucus A slippery substance produced by animals to moisten and protect body passages that are in contact with the outside world.

shrill Having a sharp, high sound.

solids Substances that have a definite shape and take up a definite amount of space.

static friction The friction that exists between two objects that are in contact but not in motion.

streamlining Designing or making something with a smooth shape that makes motion through air or water easier.

treads The ridges or grooves on the surface of a tire or on the bottom of a boot.

For More Information

Books

Boothroyd, Jennifer. *Why Do Moving Objects Slow Down? A Look at Friction* (Lightning Bolt Books). Minneapolis, MN: Lerner Publications, 2011.

Hawkins, Jay. *Push and Pull: The Science of Forces* (Big Bang Science Experiments). New York, NY: Windmill Books, 2013.

Mullins, Matt. *Friction* (A True Book). New York, NY: Children's Press, 2012.

Oxlade, Chris. *Friction and Resistance* (Fantastic Forces). Chicago, IL: Heinemann Library, 2007.

Paris, Stephanie. *Drag! Friction and Resistance* (Time for Kids Nonfiction Readers). Huntington Beach, CA: Teacher Created Materials, 2013.

Websites

Because of the changing nature of Internet links, Rosen Publishing has developed an online list of websites related to the subject of this book. This site is updated regularly. Please use this link to access the list:

http://www.rosenlinks.com/lfo/fric

INDEX